The Small Church In The Mind Of God

A NOUMENOLOGICAL PERSPECTIVE

By

Dr. Emory B. James

The Small Church In The Mind Of God

A NOUMENOLOGICAL PERSPECTIVE

By:

Dr. Emory B. James

Published By:

ABM Publications

A division of Andrew Bills Ministries, Inc.
PO Box 6811, Orange, CA 92863
www.abmpublications.com

ISBN: 978-1-931820-17-2

DEDICATION

I am grateful to my wife of 38 years,
Mrs. Venice James,

And to my children,
Emory James, Jr. & Enice James
for their encouragement who said
"Daddy You Can Do It!"

TABLE OF CONTENTS

THESIS STATEMENT

When viewed noumenologically, a church numerical value does not constitute success, nor does the size of a congregation reveal the reality of God's blessings. Viewed under the microscopic glass of the triune God, there are no small churches or large churches. God's church, even though scattered, are one, and make up the "Universal Church" in which success is measured by another yardstick, that is, "Faithfulness to God's Mandate."

> *"For my thoughts are not your thoughts,*
> *neither are your ways my ways,*
> *saith the LORD."*
> *(Isaiah 55:8 KJV)*

A Dissertation

submitted in partial fulfillment

of the requirements for the degree of

Doctor of Ministry, In the School of Ministry

Rhemalife Theological School of Ministry

February, 2014

Dr. Emory B. James

ACKNOWLEDGEMENTS

I am eternally grateful to our **Lord and Savior** for the opportunity to work and complete my Doctoral study.

I am also grateful to my **Professor, Dr. McClaurin** for tough encouragement, and for seeing in me what I didn't see in myself.

I am indebted to my **Church,** *Ephesians New Testament Church,* **and Staff** who stood by me, and understood that the "Best is Yet to Come."

I am forever grateful for the great cloud of witnesses who have encouraged me to run this race with patience looking to Jesus, the author and finisher of my Faith.

Dr. Emory B. James

FORWARD

One of the greatest deceptive entrapments today that seeks to enslave godly thinking is that a person, ministry or church is blessed based upon what they've acquired or currently possess. **"The Small Church In The Mind Of God"** will bring fresh revelation and impress on the reader the necessity of a deeper relationship with God and viewing things from a spiritual perspective.

Your soul will be awakened, informed and inspired as Dr. Emory James presents authentic spiritual truths that have either been overlooked, forgotten or discarded.

This book endeavors to share vivid insights from a spiritual perspective on how you should view things as you strive to accomplish God's mission. Being victorious through Christ Jesus isn't about physical brawn, the amount of your available resources or the number of people assembled with you. Being successful is only measured by one's obedience to our Lord.

All readers will capture the essence of how to overcome doubt and negative thinking when challenged with opposition or when things don't physically appear as prosperous as others believe it should.

Andrew Bills

Pastor/Evangelist of The Victory Report Hour International Ministries and CEO of A B M Publications.

Dr. Emory B. James

PREFACE

The Small Church in the Mind of God

By
Dr. Emory B. James

This book has been published as an encouragement to those that have been chosen by God to organize a church fellowship.

Society has decided to evaluate your successes and failure by the size of your membership and facilities. But, playing to corporate rules can be discouraging.

This book seeks to focus on the fact that God did not have a size in mind when he designed his church. God's successes are measured by a very different yardstick.

This Noumenological Perspective gives rise to understanding the perfected church, and it is not according to a size but according to mandate.

Dr. Emory B. James

INTRODUCTION

When viewed noumenologically, a church's numerical value does not constitute success, nor does the size of a congregation revea the reality of God's blessings. Viewed under the microscopic glass of the triune God, there are no small churches or large churches. God's church, even though scattered, are one, and comprise the "Universal Church" in which success is measured by another yardstick, which is, "Faithfulness to God's Mandate." However, the modern mindset is the larger the church, the more blessed it is, but the smaller it is then something must be wrong with it.

It is noteworthy to realize the church according to the government has been corporately structured, and organized. The government has given their rules as to what the structure and organizational mission of the church are within the demarcation of the society in which we live. Glenn Daman in his book, Leading the small Church states, "The mistake of the new paradigm, is that it seeks to make these corporate values normative for the church, and essential to pastoral ministry (Daman, 21). Daman indicates, as a result, truth has become minimized, and these business gurus have more to say than did theologians or Bib icists to the present church in terms of operation. In my experience, whether men call them large organization, small organizations, and medium size organizations, they all have a distinct role and influence in the communities where they exists, and more importantly their effectiveness depends on the obedience to the mandate given by God.

Jesus Christ is the Head of the church, it is His church; he ransomed it with His blood,   God has given him all authority; it stands to reason that   the members of the "Ekklesia" must function as he has designed, in regards to structure, leadership and more importantly, doctrine, and the "Great Commission. He along will bring each church to His bar of justice, and pass His final judgment on the status of His church, as seen in the book of Revelations. Therefore, this dissertation will focus on the concept of the church from a noumonological perspective, (Gods point of view).

My preoccupation with this theme began as I observed the anxiety and stress brought about due to the expectancy of "small churches" as man calls them, to grow to the level of a mega church in areas of influence and populous. However, when the idea of a small or large church is brought to the table of God's microscope for examination, it becomes apparent that there is neither a small or large church. For all Christian Churches, who believe In the death burial and resurrection and deity of Jesus Christ, are all a part of the whole or universal church. This work will prove that God does not judge a church's effectiveness by its numerical value.

Interestingly in his book, <u>Kingdom of the Cults</u>, Walter Martin quoted Dr. Bach's statement about liberal scholars who are too quick to take Gamaliel's advice. Referring to Peter and the other Apostles, Gamaliel the Pharisee said, "Refrain from these men, and let them alone; for if this counsel or this work be of men it will come to nought: But if it be of God, ye cannot overthrow it, lest you be found even to fight against God." (Acts 5:38-39)   Dr. Bach indicated that Gamaliel's advice was not biblical theology;

indicating, if it were followed in the practical realm as expressed, then we would have to recognize Islam as "of God" because of its rapid growth and reproductive virility in the world. Additionally, we would have to recognize Mormonism, which increased from six people in 1830 to over 5 million in 1982 (qt. In Martin, 13).

When we look at history, it is evident that men are mesmerized by great numbers as a symbol or power and influence, not realizing that God stated, "For my thoughts are not your thoughts, neither...my ways declares the Lord. (Isa. 55:8) It is God who gives thumbs up or thumbs down on his Church regardless of its numerical value. Man looks for numbers to deem something great in order to label it powerful, but God looks for obedience, for the triune God alone needs no one else, did not he say "I will build my Church? We must remember it was His grace that allowed man to become a part of so great a salvation, in his aloneness he needed nothing, all he needed was within himself, He created man just because he could. God reigns all by himself; Pharaoh discovered, his army was like ants in the sight of God. So it is with mega church numbers, they mean nothing to God if the church is not obedient as we discovered in the rich and powerful Laodicean Church, as also with David and Gideon's encounter with God and numbers.

Furthermore, all churches regardless of its numerical value are reminded by Jesus' statement. "Ye are the Salt of the Earth; ye are the light of the world, a city that cannot be hid."(Matt. 5:13-16) So, all churches are mandated by God to be an active, productive and effective entity in society when Jesus said, "Therefore make disciples of all men...and of the Holy Ghost. (Matt 28:19.) This work proves that God does not judge a church's effectiveness by the numbers in the pew or those on a church roll but by obedience. For Christ is the great head of the Church, who instructed us to go and make disciples of men, feed the hungry, clothe the naked, keep the faith and keep the words of the prophecy of the book of life. So pastors are to be encouraged, regardless of the size of the church, to remain faithful.

I submit to you, and am convinced, and agree with the Holy Writ, when it says, God does not see as man, His thoughts are higher. Man sees small churches, large churches, but when viewed nounmenlogically you will discover small may be big, big may be small in the eyes of Elohim. This was also suggested in the introductory pages of Tony and Felicity Dale's book, Small Is Big, when they declared, "God is shifting the Church from Church as we know it to Church-as-God wants it." Furthermore, they stated, "Real ministry can't be measured by numbers."

In this work, I will endeavor to allow you to peep into the mind of God and see noumenologically. You will come to understand why there are no small or large Churches in the sight of God. This work will endeavor to answer the question, "What is the Church?" We will examine, the concept of The Tabernacle, Temple and the Synagogue leading us to Jesus' statement regarding the eschatological aspect of its fulfillment. Again, the bigness or smallness of a Church is predicated on its obedience to the mandate given by the Great Head of the Church, the Chief Shepherd, Jesus Christ!

CHAPTER 1

Definition of
Noumenological and Phenomenology

This work will now give various definitions, firstly of the word "Noumenology," by an online expositor, Mr. Hoykes. According to Theory of Knowledge, (TOK) as defined from the great German philosopher Immanuel Kant, the "Noumenal World is the real world as opposed to the world as it appears." Hoykes indicated, Kant said of the noumenal realm, "That it cannot be known." Further, Noumenon: (Gr. ncumenon) In Kant: "An object or power transcending experience whose existence is theoretically problematic but must be postulated by practical reason. In theoretical terms Kant described the noumenon positively as "the object of a non-sensuous intuition," negatively as "not an object of the sensuous intuition;" but since he denied the existence of any but sensuous intuitions, (feel touch taste-empiricism), the noumenon remained an unknowable "X." In Kant's practical philosophy, however, the postulation of a noumenal realm is necessary in order to explain the possibility of freedom.

Hoykes explains that in the simplest sense, Kant says that there are two different worlds. The first world is called the noumenal world. It is the world of things outside us, the world of things as they are, the world of trees, dogs, cars, houses, and objects that are physically real. Furthermore, Kant points out that our minds were created in such a way that we cannot comprehend this world as it is. Instead, what we perceive is like an altered version of this world that Kant called, "the phenomenal world." The phenomenal world is the world that we perceive or to put it another way, the view we have of the world that is inside our heads. Diagrammatically, according to Kant, it might look a bit like this chart describes it.

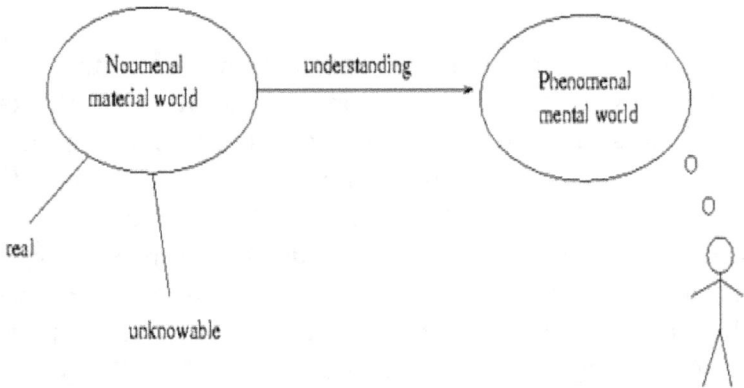

Kant States "So why doesn't information come cleanly into our heads from out there in the real world?" Hoykes writes that Kant's answer is that, a number of axioms, assumptions or rules (which he also called schema) are hard wired into our minds, and they interact with the real (noumenal) world to help create the phenomenal world that exists inside our heads. In a sense, these axioms or rules are like filters between our minds and the real world, are a bit like a man who is wearing sunglasses. The sunglasses are the schema, and they alter the way that the world really looks, to create the world that exists inside our heads, as such a man with the sunglasses on will see things as blacker or darker than they really are.

The important point is that our perceptions of the world don't just appear out of nowhere, they are caused by views from our physical surroundings. So, what that world looks like to us is a bit different to what that world is really like. The problem, however, is that while you can take off the <u>sunglasses</u> to see how bright things are, you can never take the rules, axioms, assumptions or schema out of your mind in order to find out what the world is outside your head. Hoykes explains that Kant creates an unbridgeable gap between the world out there as it really is, the noumenal world, and the world as we perceive it, the phenomenal world inside our heads.

He indicates in Kant's book, <u>Critique of Pure Reason</u>, Kant lists the 12 different axioms, assumptions or schemes that he thinks makeup the filter between our thoughts and reality. These filters aren't like sieves that remove bits and pieces of information; instead they are like concepts that we use to organize the information we receive from the world, ideas that we just can't help believing . Some of these concepts are that there is such a thing as time, such a thing as space, and such a thing as causality. While we can assume the real world is timeless, spaceless and has no causal links in it, it's impossible for us to visualize or understand this world without the concepts of time and space. They are such an integral part of the way we think, so we can't imagine how a world without them would be.

The writer suggests although the examples above concentrated on seeing, this is actually a bit misleading. Kant isn't really trying to make a point about the unreliability of perception, he is actually getting at something a bit deeper. Kant is essentially saying not that our opinions are wrong, but that the way reason acts on our perceptions alters them irrevocably, and thus it is our reason here that is acting as filter, and altering the way we view the world. That's why his axioms and assumptions are more related to concepts of reason (e.g. causality-cause and effect) than they are to elements of knowledge (e.g. blue, hot, sweet, etc.).

Hoykes questions Kant's line of reasoning by asking, "So why is this relevant to TOK? He responds, TOK is a subject that concerns itself with the pursuit of knowledge, and whether we are justified in claiming to know, what we think we know." Additionally, he states, "Kant, seems, gives us access to a real world of truths, facts, and certainties but doesn't allow us ever to know what those truths really are." I suggest because he does not know.

In the Glossary of Kant's Technical Terms, by Stephen Palmquist an online expositor, he sites noumenon as the name given to a thing when it is viewed as a transcendent object. The term negative noumenon refers only to the recognition of something which is not an object of sensible intuition, while positive noumenon refers to the attempt to know such a thing as an empirical object. In trying to understand and convey his views, Kant seems confused about the heavenly realm or kingdom.   This is obvious as he remains in a circular argument when he says "The noumenal remains an unknowable (X)." However, in his practical philosophy, the postulation of a noumenal realm is necessary in order to explain the possibility of freedom, so it remains an unknowable ("X").

Norman Geisler in his book Christian Apologetics stated, "In Kant's words, we know the phenomena, but not the noumena." Further, "There is a great impassable gulf between the real, and our knowledge of it; we must remain agnostic about reality. We know only that it is there, but can never know what it is" (qt. in Gisler-16).

How sad, of this great philosopher to know so much, but is lacking in spiritual matters.

The scriptures tells us there is a real world and it does not remain unknowable because God has revealed it through His Son Jesus Christ. Kant appears to be stunted and can't understand, why he cannot understand this veil that divides our full perception of reality, but the scriptures explain when it states, "For now we see in a mirror, dimly but then face to face" (2 Corinth, 13:12). Kant asks the question, " So why doesn't information come clearly into our heads out there in the real world." His answer is that a number of axioms, assumptions, rules and schema are hard wired into our heads and alter the way the world really looks. God has unaltered the way things look to the natural man and has given us the revelation of things eternal if one would only believe the truth. The bible said, "Pilate asked Jesus what is truth?"(John 18:38) Then Jesus answered, "I am the way, the truth, and the life...through me." (John 14:6)

To further answer Kant's question, the world of reality has been revealed. However, God reveals as much as he has seen fit. Furthermore, it is not for man to know everything, for then you become like God, and that is the area Satan continues to tempt man in God. This is seen In the garden regarding the fruit that was forbidden to eat, when he tempted Eve by stating, "For God knows that in the day you eat of it, your eyes will be opened, and you will be like God, knowing good and evil" (Gen. 3:5). God does not hold any good thing or information from us for the bible declares, "But God has revealed them to us through His Spirit. For the Spirit searches all things, yea the deep things of God." (NKJV 1 Corinth. 2:10)

The writer suggests Kant gives us access to a real world of truth, facts, and certainties but never allows us to know what those truths really are. So, I'm of the opinion that he does not know, especially when he says God is not knowable. I agree partially with that statement, God is not knowable in all aspects, but to the carnal mind he is not knowable at all, although it attests there is something out there, when in distress isn't it amazing the Anthropos know what it is, for when pain, or fear comes, the mouth cries, "Lord have mercy." The Christian belief is that God has revealed himself, through nature, through conscience, through His son Jesus Christ, and has given through the sixty six books of the bible, the embodiment of divine revelation to those who will believe.

The world of reality, the transcendent world, is prolifically seen as shown in the book of Revelation. Edward Hinson in his book Revelation Unlocking the Future stated, "A great deal has been written about whether this language in the book of Revelation, is literal, or symbolic, but what is clear is that John is describing a real place where the saved will dwell with God forever." There, we can receive a phenomenological view.

This work disagrees with Immanuel Kant when he says that the noumenal world, (Gods world) may exist, but it is utterly unknowable to humans. (qt. Wikipedia). I must pause here to address this view of agnosticism, that God is unknowable, what of the fact of his self revelation. Pascal spoke of God, as Henry Clarence Thissen declared in his book, Lectures In Systematic Theology   Thissen, stated "Pascal spoke of God as a Deus Absconditus (a hidden God), but he also held that this hidden God has revealed himself, therefore can be known." Furthermore, he states,

"Certainly one could never know God if he had not revealed himself, or communicated truth to the mind."(Thissen7). Consider the ways God has revealed himself: Through nature, the psalmist says the heavens declare the glory of God, God has revealed himself through history, his dealings with the nation of Israel and their great Egyptian deliverance, through conscience, (Rom. 2;14-16), and through his son Jesus Christ the pinnacle of that revelation.

However, Thissen states, "even philosophy did not give men a true conception of God." Additionally, Paul the Apostle writes, "In the wisdom of God the world through its wisdom did not come to know God." (1 Cor. 1-21). He further declares as Thissen indicated, that the true wisdom "none of the rulers of this age has understood; for if they had understood it, they would not have crucified the Lord of glory" (1 Cor. 2:8).

Further to define noumenology, Henry Virkler in his book, <u>Hermeneutics Principles and Processes of Biblical Interpretation</u> provides an illustration of the flood Virkler states, " It is difficult to determine from the context whether the language in Genesis 6-9 was intended to be understood noumenlogically (from God's perspective) or phenomenologically (from man's perspective), indicating that the traditional interpretation of these verses phenomenological y.

There are a plethora of meanings of these terms, when we disambiguate the word noumenlogically and phenomenologically, but for this work we are speaking about God's view of things, when referring to the word noumenlogically and man's view of things meaning phenomenologically. It is the task of this dissertation to prove this Thesis beyond doubt, so at this time after having explain the concept of noumenological, we turn briefly now to look at the definition of phenomenological.

Definition of Phenomenological

In the above definition of noumenlogically we have given an exhaustive perspective and have ruled out for this work what is the obvious, that is if noumenlogically means (from God's viewpoint), then phenomenologically mean, in regards to this work (from man's viewpoint).

Stanley Obi, an online expositor, writes that phenomenology is the primary objective of which is the direct investigation, and description of events as consciously experienced, without theories about their causal explanation and as free as possible from unexamined preconceptions and presuppositions. In conjunction, he adds, "It could be understood as the science of experienced things ranging from, seeing, hearing, touching, believing, remembering, wishing, deciding, imagining, feeling, judging and evaluating things. It is the description of the givens of immediate experience."

Stephen Hicks, in his article expresses that to understand the phenomenology, one must identify its roots in the philosophy of Immanuel Kant (1724–1804). In his Critique of Pure Reason, Kant distinguished between "phenomena" (objects as interpreted by human sensibility and understanding and "noumena") (qt. In Hicks). Objects as things-in-themselves which humans cannot directly experience, there again in my research Kant does not say what those things are. He leads us to the water but once again we cannot drink and I submit it is because the well is dry. He does not understand there is an a priori aspect to human knowledge, there is something independent of sense experience or a posteriori empiricism (what comes from experience).

In an evaluation of rationalism, Geisler at least indicates, "There must be an a priori dimension to knowledge...but there must be at least some natural inclinations of the mind toward truth or the first principle of knowledge, if not nothing could ever be known. Geisler indicated "If all knowledge came through the senses, it could not be known as true by the senses." Additionally, Geisler writes, "there may be nothing in the mind that was not first in the senses, except the mind itself. Consequently, he surmises that the mind must possess some innate or natural abilities of its own to engage in the pursuit of truth. He suggests this concept is essential to any realistic epistemology." (Geisler 42).

According to the bible, there is something contrary to Kant's theory, that all knowledge come from the senses, and are not innate or a priori. However, the bible speaks of knowledge that comes from another source, when speaking of Gentiles who do not have the law but obey or disobey the natural law of conscience the bible says, "In that they show the works of the Law written in their hearts, their conscience bearing witness and their thoughts alternately accusing or else defending them." (Rom. 2:15 NASB). What of "tacit knowledge?" it does not come from the senses, I want be long on this point, but according to Wikipedia encyclopedia, something that's difficult to write down or visualize, or transfer from one person to another cannot be written with words.

1. How to speak a language
2. Innovation is an illusive skill
3. Leadership is difficult to teach, no training can guarantee to make one a leader
4. Body language is difficult to teach
5. Humor, it's not always possible to explain why something is funny

What I am saying is that all knowledge does not come from your experience, something's we just know. We know how to call on God, even if one is an atheist when extreme pain is a presence. The idea of noumenology, and phenomenology has been successfully defined. We will refer in this dissertation, to noumenologically meaning from (God's perspective and phenomenologically from (Man's perspective). We now turn our attention to the phemenological and noumenological view of the church.

Phemenological View of the Church

Webster dictionary: The term Christian Church, when used as a proper noun usually refers to the whole Christian religious tradition throughout history. When used in this way the term does not refer to a particular denomination or to a building. However, the majority of Christians belong to groups that consider themselves to be the one true Church. The three largest such groups are the Roman Catholic Church, the Eastern Orthodox Church, and the Oriental Orthodox communion. Thus, some Christians identify the Christian Church with a visible structure (the view of the Roman Catholic, Eastern Orthodox and Oriental Orthodox churches).

Others understand it as an invisible reality not identified with any earthly structure, (the general Protestant view) and others equate it with particular groups that share certain essential elements of doctrine, and practice though divided on other points of doctrine and government (such as the branch theory as taught by some Anglicans). The IRS has its definition for the word church in it's pamphlet, Guide for Churches and Religious Organizations their glossary, gives the definition of a church as:

> Certain characteristics are generally attributed to churches. These attributes of a church have been developed by the IRS and by court decisions . They include: distinct legal existence; recognized creed and form of worship; definite and distinct ecclesiastical government; formal code of doctrine and discipline; distinct religious history; membership not associated with any other church or denomination; organization of ordained ministers; ordained ministers selected after completing prescribed courses of

study; literature of its own; established places of worship; regular congregations; regular religious services; Sunday schools for the religious instruction of the young; schools for the preparation of its ministers. The IRS generally uses a combination of these characteristics, together with other facts and circumstances, to determine whether an organization is considered a church for federal tax purposes. The IRS makes no attempt to evaluate the content of whatever doctrine a particular organization claims is religious, provided the particular beliefs of the organization are truly and sincerely held by those professing them and the practices and rites associated with the organization's belief or creed are not illegal or contrary to clearly defined public policy.

Noumenological View of the Church

Just what is the Church? According to an online expositor, Phil Laspino, he indicates the word church is derived from the Greek word, "Kuriakon." Laspino stated, "Church is that which belongs to or is appropriated to the Lord."

Additionally, he added that it may be a German word meaning, "to elect, choose out," therefore, corresponding to the Greek ("ekklesia") meaning an assembly called together. The most popular definition is that the church is understood to be the collective body of Christians, or all those who profess to believe in Christ, acknowledging him as the Savior.

The Introductory Study Guide: <u>Understanding Ministry</u> by **Dennis McCallum** and **Gary DeLashmutt** as reported by Xenos organization online, indicates the word translated "church" in the English Bible is <u>ecclesia.</u> This word is the Greek words <u>kaleo</u> (to call), with the prefix <u>ek</u> (out). Thus, the word means "the called out ones." However, they clarify an important fact that the English word "church" does not come from ecclesia but from the word kuriakon, which means "dedicated to the Lord." Additionally, this word was commonly used to refer to a holy place or temple. By the time of Jerome's translation of the New Testament from Greek to Latin, it was customary to use a derivative of kuriakon to translate ecclesia.

It is interesting to note the article said the word church is a poor translation of the word ecclesia since it implies a sacred building, or temple. A more accurate translation would be "assembly" because the term ecclesia was used to refer to a group of people who had been called out to a meeting. It was also used as a synonym for the word synagogue, which also means to "come together," i.e. a gathering of the "Body of Christ" Since believers have been united with Christ through spiritual baptism, they are sometimes corporately referred to as the body of Christ. (Rom. 12:4-5; 1 Cor. 12:11,13,18,27; Col. l:l8; Eph. 5:30)

The idea seems to be that the group of Christians in the world constitute the physical representation of Christ on earth. It is also a metaphor which demonstrates the interdependence of members in the church, while at the same time demonstrating their diversity from one another. (Rom. 12:4; 1 Cor. 12:14-17).

We have looked at man's view of the church as opposed to God's view. However, it's of paramount importance that we further consider what Jesus stated regarding the church when he said, "Upon this rock I will build my church." (Matt. 16:18). There have been several buildings throughout history. The Tabernacle, the Temple and the Synagogue which have all served their purpose, but what is this church that Jesus promises to build, this work will examine its scope, with a view to its eschatological concept. Arthur Ritchie, a bible scholar, indicated that, the Temple was a fixed and permanent structure located at Jerusalem. The word "Temple" carries with it rich meaning as understood in the Greek context. We must consider two Greek words: "naos" and "hieron." These words are wrapped up in the fact that wherever God dwells, that is his temple. (qt. In McClaurin's dissertation)

Jesus indicated it would be His Church. It had nothing to do with a size initially, but I submit to you he was talking about the Universal Church. In this section we will consider, Church universal, Church militant, Church triumphant, noticing the oneness as oppose to the size. It stands to reason if the triune God is one that he would want his church to be one. God declared to Israel, "Yis'ra'eil Adonai Eloheinu Adonai Echad" being interpreted, (Hear, Israel, the Lord is our God, the Lord is One. (Deut. 6:4-9 KJV) Would you not say dear reader, if

God is one, would he want His Church divided into small and large? Jesus states, "And other sheep I have, which are not of this fold: them also I must bring, and they shall hear my voice; and there shall be one fold, and one Shepherd.(John 10:16)

John on the Isle of Patmos records God showed him this great undivided Church. He states, "After this I beheld, and lo a great multitude which no man could number, of all nations, and kindreds" (Rev. 7-9) I submit to you he was talking about the universality of the people of God. The Church Universal is one, not divided into small or large, but when viewed noumenologically, it is one Church.

Church Universal

It is imperative that the concept of the Universal Church then be explained by first asking the question, "Where did it come from?" An examination of Christian Theology and Systematic Theology will clear this concept. According to Millard and Thissen in their research, concluded that Christian Theology is the enterprise that seeks to construct a coherent system of Christian belief and practice. This is based primarily upon the texts of the Old Testament and the New Testament, as well as the historical traditions of Christians.

Christian theologians use biblical exegesis, rational theology which might be undertaken to help the theologian better understand Christian tenets, make comparisons between Christianity and other traditions. It is used to defend Christianity against objections and criticism, facilitate reforms in the Christian church, assist in the propagation of Christianity, draw on the resources of the Christian tradition to address some present situation or need and or for a variety of other reasons.

Systematic theology, according to Thissen, is a discipline of Christian theology that formulates an orderly, rational, and coherent account of the Christian faith and beliefs. Systematic theology draws on the foundational sacred texts of Christianity while simultaneously investigating the development of Christian doctrine over the course of history, particularly through philosophical evolution. Millard J. Erickson, in her book <u>Christian Theology</u>, states that, "It draws upon the whole of the Bible, rather than utilizing individual texts in isolation from one another." (21) Additionally, theology must be contemporary, she writes, "While it treats timeless issues, it must use language, concepts, and thought forms that make sense in the context of the present time. She warns of "modernizing Jesus" (22).

Millard writes, "Among the reasons why the church must strive for unity are didactic passages in that the most persuasive proof is "the so call high priestly prayer of Jesus, when he said, "I do not pray for these only, but also for those who believe in me through their words that they may be one, even as thou hast love me." (John 17:20-23) Many scriptures attest to the Universal Church: Eph. 4:4-16, 1 Cor:12:13.

The Universal Church derives its definition from the baptizing ministry of the Holy Spirit. The key verse on this is 1 Cor. 12:13, "By <u>one</u> Spirit we are all baptized into <u>one</u> body." From this passage the Church is the physical manifestation of Christ, i.e., his body. Other passages that use the same imagery are Rom. 12:4-5; 1 Cor. 12:11,18,27.

The point in all of these passages seems to be that anyone who has experienced this baptism is automatically a member of the body of Christ.

David Horton in his book, The Portable Seminary states, "When speaking of the nature of the church, it holds a bold view regarding the way the Apostle Paul spoke of the whole, and local church: "Thus it is not the addition of churches that make the whole church, nor is the whole church divided into separate congregations, but wherever the church meets, she exists as a whole, she is a church in that place. The particular congregation represents the Universal Church, and through participation in Christ's redemption, mystically comprehends the whole of which it is a local manifestation."

Horton concludes that the New Testament speaks of the Church as God's building, [however he left out the fact, that of the building, Jesus was the Chief Cornerstone] His planting, vineyard, temple, household, olive tree, city, and His people."(Horton, 185). Additionally, in this discussion, Horton alludes to the fact that although we are all baptized into the one Body of Christ, each has been given a special function. He stated, "At the same time her lord, her judge, her bridegroom, her life, her holiness and her unity in him. (Horton, 185). Thus this work will presents Church Universal, Church Militant, Church Triumphant, and will take a close look at postmodernism and the emergent church, leading to discover that the church as we know it is evolving to the Eschatology Church. Let look at the two divisions of the Universal Church. In Christian theology, the Christian Church, or Church Universal, is traditionally divided into two:

The Church Militant (Ecclesia Militans)

Church Militant, Comprises Christians on earth who are living, and who struggle against sin, the devil and "..the rulers of the darkness of this world, against spiritual wickedness in high places" (Ephesians 6:12).

The Church Triumphant (Ecclesia Triumphans)

Horton stated, "the heavenly Church is the bride awaiting Christ her bridegroom," furthermore, since Christ loved the church and gave himself up for her, and cleansed her by the washing of water with the word, he is now sanctifying her for the marriage feast of the lamb. (Horton, 186). Although Christians may be physically separated from each other by the barrier of death, they nonetheless remain united to each other in one Church and support each other in prayer. According to the Bible, "We are compassed about with so great a cloud of witnesses (Heb. 12;1). The souls cry that are under the altar, how long?

Local Church/Church militant

What is the local church? In this discussion students were asked to describe the scope or area encompassed by each of the following references. The point is that in each reference, the word "Church" is in the singular. Since the scope of what is meant by each reference is different, we can draw conclusions about what constitutes a local church. During the question and answer discussion several things were revealed regarding the church. They were instructed to indicate "What geographical area is being described in the following verses?"

1.   Col. 1:18

2.   Acts 9:31

3.   1 Cor. 1:2

Answers:

1. Col. 1:18 -the church throughout the world

2. Acts 9:31 - the church throughout a region

3. 1 Cor. 1:2- the church in a city (compare 14:34)

Question: What implications can we draw from these four passages concerning what size or structure a group must have to be considered a local church?

Answer: The word "Church" is not a technical designation of a local group of any particular size or structure. Instead, it apparently describes any extent of locality under discussion. Therefore, in answer to the question, "What constitutes a local church?" The scriptural answer is that any part of the Universal Church, which is somehow local, can be said to be a local church.

We would suggest this boils down to the level where "Two or three have gathered together in my name (Mt. 18:20). This seems to be Christ's version of what is necessary to have a local church. In the first and second century, Christians worshipped in private homes, fields, or remote areas. They were not recognized by the Roman state or the religious Jews. If caught they would be taken in for questioning, may have been tortured, put in prison or even killed. It was not until the late third or fourth century that Christians began to worship the Lord in public places, without fear. Sometimes several conditions, such as the proper observation of the sacraments, the presence of duly established clergy, a formal government and ministry to all ages were given before a group can be called a church. What might be the motive for constructing such added conditions? I verge to say for man's purposes.

Tabernacles, Temples , Synagogue

In order to trace a motif showing that religion has always had its holy place and found its expression in tangible edifices, we will now consider the tabernacle temple and synagogue, with the intention of showing they all were leading up to the church as we know it. Fulfilling a divine purpose the shifting got closer to the eschatological church, finally realizing that wherever God dwells is His temple. The church has not fully come to grips with Paul's statement according to 1 Corinthians 6:19 "What know ye not that your body is the temple of The Holy Ghost."

According to   Dr. W.M. McClaurin's dissertation, The Issue of Rebuilding the Temple in Jerusalem she points out that the Tabernacle was the center of the Israelites' worship for five hundred years, from Moses to David, until Solomon's temple was built. The lesson from the tabernacle still lingers, serve your purpose weather your storms, and when you have completed your work, God will retire you.

The Temple

The Temple was a fixed and permanent structure, expressed Lionel Ritichie, an online writer, further when choosing a Greek word for Temple, Naos rather than Hieron is used, safeguarding the fact that God's Temple was not made with hands (Acts 17:24). As defined by Studylight, an online article, Hieron, referred primarily to the visible structure while Naos had typological reference to the Tabernacle in the wilderness (qt. in McClaurin diss). These religious buildings to include the church, were never meant to compete with one another, but each had a purpose pointing to the unity of the people of God and were judged not by their size or pomp in society, but by their faithfulness to the mandate of God. I have included a list of denomination and their origins in the back of this work.

Synagogue

After the Temple was destroyed by the Babylonians in 586 B.C, the people still needed a place to worship. The synagogue came into being and became the Jewish house of worship. It was a designated building or place used by the Jews for "gathering together." Later, Jesus himself was found teaching in these synagogues, (Matt. 4:23-9:35).

According to McClaurin, the building of the Temple was God's idea. He complained about not having a house of Cedar (2 Sam.7:7). However, the Temple and the Tabernacle had another purpose. Its short term purpose was to build God a sanctuary, but the long term purpose was to arouse the people of God to look to the Promised Messiah who would fulfill every picture of the tabernacle. McClaurin explained, "Jesus Christ was the true tabernacle and the true temple. So complete was the incarnation, that the unity of God with his people in the tabernacle must fade into insignificance. For when Christ came there was no longer a need for the shadowy worship of the temple. The physical had to give way to the authentic." This work will now look at the last Temple.

The Eschatological Temple

In God's kingdom there is a Temple, however John said he saw no Temple in the New Jerusalem.(Rev. 21:22) I would surmise from the biblical text, no Temple, no Tabernacle, no Church. no big or small, no more denomination. Paradoxical as it might sound the fact is, there will be no need for religious buildings, [that's a scary thought for some who are used to their elaborate mega buildings they could brag on]. For Jesus and God will usher in the Eschatological Temple, for they are the new Temple and their glory will light the city. In the Eschatological Temple, God will rule in the hearts of men. It is amazing; Jesus is the Eschatological Temple (John 2:13-22). His glory will shine, not the little concept of man's version of the Church.

Regarding the Church, many have asked, "Can we know for sure what the church is and does the church mandate matter?" We will discuss relativism, postmodernism and the emergent church, to obtain a coherent view regarding "absolutes," God's mandate and criteria for the church to be a church. Is it numerical value that God is looking? Is it a beautiful edifice? What defines the bigness or smallness of a church when one looks nomenologically? This work will turn now and examine two of the seven Churches in Asia Minor.

Chapter 2

A Noumenological Evaluation
Of Two Churches

So many ask the question, how does God see his church today? What is the main factor in the mind of God when he looks at the church? Briefly we will look at two of the seven churches to further prove this Thesis that God does not see as man, and he judges the church not by size but obedience. The two churches commended with no rebuke were Smyrna and Philadelphia. Both were small, poor and lacked influence, but they were faithful in their confession. There is no indication that these churches were growing, since they had existed for some length of time and yet were small. Neither would not have been great church growth success cases.

The Philadelphia Church

The Philadelphia Church, according to the bible, God was pleased with it He says to the church, "Because you have kept My command to persevere, I also will keep you from the hour of trial which shall come upon the whole world, to test those who dwell on the earth." (Rev. 3:7-13). This church was small by the world standard, but Church growth from God's point of view is when a church is faithful to God's mandate, consider what was also said to this church, by God " I know your works, I have set before you an open door, and no one can shut it; for you have a little strength, have kept My word, and have not denied my name" (Rev. 3:8)

This statement is evident that Jesus walks in the midst of His Church all the time; He looks to see where we are spiritually, not where we are numerically. The Philadelphian Church works were Christ centered; their ministry was dedicated wholly unto the Lord; they were listening to the voice of God as he spoke, and God placed before them, according to the Bible an <u>open door</u> into the very presence of God. (Rev. 3:8) He describes her outward condition in the world, poor it was, but rich in faith.

The Church in Laodicea

The Laodicea Church was very successful, but it was rebuked. Although it was rich, with no membership problem, in God sight it was small, unhealthy, naked and spiritually weak. In <u>Haley's Handbook of The Bible</u> it stated that, "The lukewarm Church of Laodicea was a banking center proud of its wealth, beautified with resplendent temples and theatres." (584). One would surely think this is the Church, large, beautiful and popular, but look what God said to this church, "I know thy works, that thou art neither cold nor hot: I would thou wert cold or hot. So then because thou art lukewarm, and neither cold or hot, I will spew thee out of my mouth. Because thou saith I am rich and increased with goods, and have need of nothing; and knoweth not that thou are wretched, and miserable and poor and blind and naked" (Rev. 3:17-18). O dear reader, that we would see phenomenologically through the eyes of God! Truly small can be broad and massive as is evident with these churches. It can be small even, though in man's sight it's large and rich with great wealth, but lacking in richness towards God. It is not the outward appearance that the Lord judges; it's the inward spirit of power afforded to each that must be maintained and illuminated in order to grow His church.

The Emerging Church and Postmodernism

There are a few terms we need to define: Postmodernism, what is it? Matt Slick, an excellent writer, states that, "Postmodernism is not that simple to define because it is a word used in different areas of study: art, film, architecture, literature, religion, truth." The term "postmodernism" is best understood by relating it to modernism. According to Slick, this innovation came out of the 1800's of Western Europe with the manifestation of the mechanism, industrialism, progress, literature, art, and the ideas that sought to capitalize on what promoted a progressive and prosperous society. It elevated human reason, human progress, and human authority.

Postmodernism, then, is not necessarily a rebellion against modernism (though some postmodernists see it that way), but a movement "after" it, a movement that builds upon it but, more or less, rejects modernism's strict reasoning. In contrast to this, postmodernism upholds a subjectivity regarding morality, social constructions, political movements, art, religion and truth statements, to oversimplify what postmodernism is. Slick suggests it's the belief that truth is relative, that objective truth is not visible. Furthermore, Slick points out modernism is often pictured as pursuing truth, absolutism, linear thinking, rationalism, certainty, the cerebral as opposed to the effective, which in turn breeds arrogance, and inflexibility, the lust to be right, the desire to control. Postmodernism, by contrast, recognizes how much of what we 'know' is shaped by the culture in which we live, is controlled by emotions, esthetics, heritage, and, in fact, can only be intelligently held as part of a common tradition, without overbearing claims to be true or right.

The danger of postmodernism is that it tends to deny the ability to know things for sure. [can't we know 2+2=4 or what goes up must come down? We can know there is a God]. However, postmodernism undermines the construction of language by stating that words can be interpreted differently, that language is fluid and that the Bible, written in ancient languages, is open to various interpretations of equal validity. Given this underlying idea that nothing is truly knowable, the very foundations of truth both moral and spiritual are suspect and open to re-evaluation along with the Bible.

Slick says the majority of unbelievers do not have even a basic understanding of biblical principles. Their worldview is often naturalistic; that is, they perceive and interpret the world in light of natural principles (often evolutionary), combined with relativism in the areas of morals and truth. The postmodern person says truth is understood in the context of one's culture and personal experience and these observations in turn dominate how the world is interpreted rather than an objective absolute truth; i.e., God's revelation. The individual observes and accepts what he considers to be true and false based upon his experiences. Different cultures and different individuals will interpret reality differently. In other words, what is true for one person may not be true for another. Pilate asked Jesus, "What is truth?" Jesus answered, "I am the way, the truth and the life." God has fixed it so that there is not a truth for you or a truth for me, we are all subjected to God's truth for men everywhere.

Jesus speaks of the two roads, two gates and only two paths. He speaks of the wide and the narrow road, the straight gate and that only one road leads to life eternal. (Matt 7:13-14) In the Tabernacle there was only one door to enter, symbolizing Jesus' statement, "I am the door" (John 10:9). What does this prove, it proves the oneness of the church, no small or large, but one Universal Church.

Concluding from an earlier Barna study, David Kinnaman, President of The Barna Group, noted that most Americans do not have strong and clear beliefs mainly because they do not possess a coherent biblical worldview.

The study found that fewer Americans were embracing a traditional view of God and the Bible. **Sighting that**, the postmodern person rejects the biblical absolutes, that there is an immutable God; that God is sovereign and that the only way to salvation is through the blood sacrifice of Jesus. Therefore, the Christian and the postmodern person often do not have sufficient common ground to allow proper dialogue on spiritual matters. The postmodern person might ask if there is any such thing as truth and whether or not truth can be known either experientially or rationally. The modernist would say, "Of course there is absolute truth! Asking if truth can be known is an absolute question!"

Generally speaking, those in the Emerging Church movement are aware of the postmodern mindset and admirably seek to adapt evangelistic efforts to accommodate postmodern thinking. Sometimes this means that some Emerging Churches will feature church services and emphasize relationship, community and typical traditional values while using visual methods, storytelling and more expressive worship instead of absolute truth constructions derived from scripture and delivered during preaching and teaching.

Emerging Churches use paintings, slides, drawings, and candles as visual expressions. In addition, they might show videos or television clips. On occasion, even an art installation or exhibit may function in place of an entire service. This work agrees with the research. We must reach the culture in a relevant way, a way with which they are familiar. We must also make sure that we do not compromise the revealed word of God, and we must not let the revealed truth of God's Word be subjugated to cultural or personal pressures. Jesus said, "Upon this rock I will build my church and the gates of hell shall not prevail against it" I am of the opinion, man must look to Jesus not modern equipment, the choir, the musical instruments nor the flashy pulpits. For it is Christ who will send laborers into the vineyard when the church seeks God and prays.

Postmodernism is relativism. Postmodernism is a reaction against the logical truth structures of modern thought that gave us absolute propositions about nature, time, space, mathematics, knowability, repeatability of experimentation, predictability, etc. There are always people who ask questions rather than blindly follow the status quo. They look for different ways of expression, different interpretations of truth, teach the idea that truth is not necessarily absolute and that reality can be reinterpreted. It is within the postmodern context that the Emerging Churches are seeking to work. The word of God has established the absolutes for the church: It is one, He will build it. Its growth is in prayer; its success with God is not its size or beautiful, large edifices but its faithfulness to the "Great Commission." It seems as if some pastors are competing when they say, "Dr. what's your membership?" How big was the crowd? How much did you raise?

So, Instead of complete truth propositions, Emerging Churches tend to focus on relationships, expressiveness and new ways of trying to reach God. Is it good? Yes and no. It is good only so far as it is consistent with Scripture. It is bad whenever it deviates from it. A further definition of relativism, for more precise meaning; because it is within the postmodern context, according to Slick is that the emerging churches are seeking to work. Relativism says there is no absolute truth. However, we know the word of God is true, we know that the grave was empty and that Jesus got up because he was seen by many, it is true no one has ever found his body.

Dr. Emory B. James

Chapter 3

A Noumenological View of Numbers

God does not depend on a large number of people to achieve His goals. I submit to you that a church might be numerically small, but God can take a few and accomplish His purpose as seen in two biblical characters: David and Gideon. Why then did David number Israel?

David

1st Chronicles 21:1-4

- "And Satan stood up against Israel, and provoked David to number Israel.

- And David said to Joab and to the rulers of the people, "Go, number Israel from Beersheba even to Dan; and bring the number of them to me, that I may know it.

- And Joab answered, "The LORD make his people an hundred times so many more as they be: but, my lord the king, are they not all my lord's servants? Why then doth my lord require this thing? Why will he be a cause of trespass to Israel?"

- Nevertheless the king's word prevailed against Joab. Wherefore Joab departed, and went throughout all Israel, and came to Jerusalem."

The first thing we should glean from this episode is that it was Satan who provoked David to number Israel. In other words, numbering Israel's army was done because the adversary Satan was tempting David. That is a crucial thing to remember because it explains much. The second thing to consider is David's reason for doing this was, "that he may know it." In other words, his own delight or pleasure was what induced him to do this. These are the keys towards understanding this sin. <u>God</u> allowed David to be tempted by Satan because Israel had taken their eyes off God as their ruler, fortress and provider.

By illustrating his confidence in the number of his own soldiers, rather than trust in the Lord, he illustrated the sin of Israel. The census was merely a product of the sin of God's people in that they fell away from trusting in their God. Tony Warren, a theologian points out reasons for David counting his soldiers and that counting can be done for good reasons or wrong reasons. So based upon all the available biblical information, David did his counting because of the human ego and pride. He wanted to determine how powerful Israel's army was.. A modern day analogy would be in Christians becoming gratified in thinking too highly of themselves for what they have become, for how many converts they had made, or for how successful the congregation had become under their guidance. Warren stated, "It is not the will of the Father that we glory in our own strength or power, but that we depend upon Him and glory in His power."

We triumph in the work of His hands, glory in the power of His arm and by the strength of His will. Any other motivation to delight or have pleasure in our numbers is the temptation of the flesh. Israel's greatness and power were all by God's hand, God's presence, and God's blessings. God loved David, and Israel, but they temporarily forgot this. According to the Bible, God chastises those whom He loves. Have you heard this saying, "Doctor, how many members do you have?" David sinned in his pleasure in possessing a great army. He was counting his soldiers to the glory of Israel, instead of the glory of the Lord. As a representative of Israel, in him was shown their confidence in their own arm for their help. This caused God to pronounce and deliver them into judgment. We cannot believe in big or small churches but the Lord.

This work is crystal clear, that numbers do not hinder the plan of God. Tony Warren, an online teacher asks the question, "Why did David number Israel? And why was it a sin that King David numbered Israel?" Warren says, David's sin must be understood in the light of the entire context of Israel. When all these things are searched out and considered in light of the whole Bible, Warren stated, "I believe that David's sin is revealed to be the chronic sin of Israel, which was, pride and vanity." We hear it today, Dr. how large is your church?   I will not prolong this point, I think this thesis has proven in David's life that numbers do not impress God as they do men.   Consider the scripture from:

Isaiah 31:1

> • "Woe to them that go down to Egypt for help; and stay on horses, and trust in chariots, because they are many; and in horsemen, because they are very strong; but they look not unto the Holy One of Israel, neither seek the LORD!"

God doesn't want our strength to be in numbers but in Him.

Gideon

To further prove numbers, and size is not of foremost important to God, we now turn to examine God's dealing with Gideon. According to The Expository Files by John W. Quinn, Gideon was the fifth judge of Israel. He played a small but significant role in the history of God's people. Many theologians believed Gideon lived during a time when Israel had forsaken God and had worshipped idols. The nation had abandoned its real source of national strength and the source of its benefits, much like our own society has done today. God had withdrawn his blessings and protection, and the country had suffered. As voices began to call upon God for deliverance, God used Gideon to answer the need. Gideon was a reluctant leader who was finally convinced of the power of God. He ultimately led the children of Israel in victory over their enemies, the Midianites.

Quinn indicated after God called Gideon, and Gideon had been persuaded to accept the task God gave him. We find the account of Gideon's defeat of the Midianites in Judges 7:1-8:21. Gideon's army of 32,000 was reduced in size (vs. 1-8). Already sorely outnumbered (the enemy numbered over 120,000 swordsmen), most would see this as a time to go out and recruit more warriors. But it might be that after the victory the Lord would give them, the people might think it had been by their own strength and ability that they had won the victory. So, the Lord commanded Gideon to further reduce the number under his command "...lest Israel claim glory for itself...saying, 'My own hand has saved me.'" (Judges 7:2). Any who were "afraid and trembling" were told they could go home.

Some 22,000 departed leaving 10,000 to fight the Midianites. So, it went from being outnumbered 4 to 1 to being outnumbered 12 to 1.

According to the Bible, "Then the Lord said to Gideon, 'The people are still too many; bring them down to the water, and I will <u>test</u> them for you there." (Judges 7:4). The Bible indicates that there was drinking water at the site that the Lord had directed him to. The army stopped to drink and 9,700 knelt down on their knees so they might drink directly from the stream. The other 300 cupped their hands and took water into them, drinking it from their hands as a dog would lap water from <u>his</u> bowl. "The LORD said to Gideon, 'I will deliver you with the 300 men who lapped and will give the Midianites into your hands; so let all the other people go, each man to his home.'" (Judges 7:7).

God does not need tremendous number to accomplish His purpose. The Lord has often demonstrated His power by taking a few and accomplishing His purpose. Pastors don't be afraid of being in the minority if that is what it takes to be right with God!

Dr. Emory B. James

Chapter 4

A Noumenological Perspective
Of Two Or Three

A church of two or three may not be a very good church in that it is not able to fulfill all of the functions that are appropriate for a local church according to the New Testament, but this does not mean that it is not a church. A distinction must be made between that which determines the "being" of the church versus the "well-being" of the church.

In his book, Unleashing the Potential Of The Smaller Church, Shawn McMullen stated, "I'm glad in the last few years we've heard more about church health and less about church growth. True, healthy churches grow," however, he indicated that church growth is necessary and states, "But who determines when a church is growing and when it is not?"

He continues by asking the question, is there more to church growth than meets the eye? McMullen concluded by showing only God grows the Church, he appears to agree with this argument by indicating that God alone evaluates growth. McMullen makes the observation, small or large we are a part of a vast, innumerable multitude on earth a multitude of believers and churches, and collectively with all the other saints and churches around the world. He further agrees with this argument in concluding that God's Church is doing something substantial and that the Church collectively is a part of the big picture. (McMullen 152-153)

Jesus stated, something profound, "For where two or three are gathered together in my name I am there among them. (NIV. Matt. 18:20) Is He saying something about the church size noumenologically? I mean if God is in the midst of two or three, how big can that be, so we propose to you, there must be a spiritual way to measure bigness in eternity that we must grasp. I suggest our sights are too low; we do not yet understand the language of the Spirit.

The Concept of the Small Church

Where does the idea come from that if a church is small it's not being blessed or it's not successful? To be fair, we want to look at the idea of a so-called small church phenomenologically. What does a man mean by the phrase "small church?" The small church in America is defined as any worship assembly with less than 100 members gathering together. That being the case, many would believe that the ability to serve would be limited and the mandate would be reduced. However, I submit to you that God's command to go into all the world and preach yet remains; and size is not a deterrent.

Many have discussed the vicissitude of the concept of small, in regards to the numerical strength. However, as we continue to develop and prove this thesis, we will see in the illustration of two biblical characters, namely David and Gideon and that God's nature is to use less to accomplish His purposes. You may ask why? The answer and the truth of the matter is; He needs nothing or no one. He includes man because we are workers together with

Him. In the scheme of things, whatever is accomplished, it's God working behind the scenes.

Consider if you will, if a church grows numerically or does not grow, it's all the Lord's doing, it's not the innovative equipment, the church growth strategy. Does God need help? Consider the statement, "I will build my church." Further, when one is allowed by God to see noumonologically, you will realize the impact of Jesus' statement when He said. "Upon this rock I will, build my church and the gates of ...against it." Can't you see if the Church grows numerically God is growing it. If it does not grow numerically God is not allowing it, for His purposes. Did he not say, even the gates of hell would not be able to prevail against it?

By man's standard big is blessed, small is less, but I submit to you regarding the church, smallness or largeness in God mathematics has nothing to do with the size. You will discover that small can be large. and large can be small. Tony and Felicity Dale/George Barna agree with this idea, in their book, Small Is Big. I know this is paradoxical language, but none the less real.

Did not our Lord say our ways are not his way, nor our thoughts his thought? We must also consider that the disobedient church will not stand, but for awhile. The bigness of the Church does not mean it's blessed of God. Jim Jones had an extensive following. The Muslim Church, the Mormon Church and Buddhists all have large followings and are considered cults. There must be another standard, as this work will prove when it take into consideration two of the seven churches, in the book of Revelation. I have chosen these two because of their contrasting positions, and God's evaluation of them. It will become crystal clear that this argument is correct and we have not dealt in relativism, but absolute and the objective truth of God for His church.

Further, when we consider the order of the church, size has nothing to do with it. The mandate is to go, and make disciples of men. The Bible is clear as to the mandate of the Ekklesia or the called out ones, church size did not matter, What mattered was obedience to the call, they met from house to house maintaining the doctrine of message, which was Christ death, resurrection, and return as noted in (Acts 2:46). In conjunction, the Christian Church is commanded by Christ to go ye in all the world and preach the Gospel...of men (Matt. 28:19-20). The concept of small and large regarding the church is man's terminology. To God it's just the "Church." Note dear reader, when He writes to the seven churches in the book of Revelation, He does not say; "to the small church in Sardis or to the large church in Laodicea." Notice the language in the eschatological book where it is written, "To the Church" (Rev.2:29, 3:22).

Inadequate Views of Success

Damon, states, "Nowhere have cultural perspectives had a greater impact on the church than in the perception of what it takes to be a successful leader. No one enters the pastorate with the view of becoming a failure. All pastors strive to attain success and feel incredibly guilty if they come up short. They wonder if they should blame themselves for not working harder, praying more, or being more skilled at ministry. Or maybe if their congregations were more open to new ideas." (26)   Damon further indicates that these inadequate views of success have done much to skew the pastoral role and leads to disillusion.

It's interesting to note that the church comes in all shapes, sizes and ethnicities. In noting this, one should take into consideration that the church is about community and social identity. As families migrated to this country, bringing many traditions and cultural influences, these forces based on social identification, brought their own religious customs. In order to be comfortable socially they organized their own churches. As this was done it gave rise to the idea of forming reformations so that wherever these communities settled, they could find a socially comfortable worship experience. What that said was that the size of that church was governed by the number of those that the community was ethnically connected to.

On the other hard, in a research entitled, The Faulty Promises of the Church Growth Movement, by Bob De Waay, he contradicts the above statement by quoting Ralph Elliot when he states, " I agree with Elliot. The outcome based approach that judge results by numbers assures that churches will go where there are homogenous units."

Further, the question is: are we becoming Christians or are we about building institutional membership? This question is powerful and thought provoking, indeed! Additionally, he writes, if one tailors the church to identify with its culture, and engage in pseudo-gospel of possibility thinking, will the results bear any similarity to the church? He continues; the church consists of the "called out ones" not those who enjoy having a religious experience with people who are just like themselves.

True fellowship is not the gathering of religious consumers with similar felt needs, but it's the fellowship around the person and work of Jesus Christ (1 John 1:3, 6,7). This is not true Christian fellowship, it's something else. The Greek word describes it [heteros] [another kind] rendering this another kind of friendship or association, but not the one described in 1 John 1, [(allos)] meaning [the same kind.] After Elliot refutes the church growth strategy of lumping "like people" together we will now consider Daman's theory on three things that he feels attributes to the growth of the so-called small church. Is this truth objective, subjective or no truth at all? Daman's three thought areas are:

1. What was the effectiveness of community outreach? To evaluate the effects, one must look at the goals of leadership. That goal must be the effect by the preaching of the Gospel. The mistake in the past has been that we thought the church could be transformed through vision casting, mission statements, program growth and organizational structures. Although, each of these elements has its own place, we have often overlooked the first and most important element – the biblical mandate to preach the Word. When Paul encountered a spiritual unhealthy church, he did not develop a five-step renewal program or recast the church's organizational vision. Instead, he confronted the issues through the development of a biblical theology. The Church at Corinth was in deep spiritual trouble. It had allowed sin to go

unchecked; it was devastated by divisions and immorality, and it refused to submit to authority. But rather than coming in and reorganizing the church, Paul made it clear that the key to spiritual transformation was the preaching of the scriptures" (Daman, 135).

2.   What was the influence of the ministry within the community? To address the question, I will explore the discussion shared in the book, Unleashing the Potential of the Smaller Church, by Shawn McMullen. There is a principle discussed in light of the action taken by a Puritan minister by the name of Richard Baxter. It seemed that Baxter was sent to a small town by the name of Kidderminster, Worcestershire, England that had little or no interest in the Church.   Rev. Baxter had a compassion for preaching and preached as he had never preached before. This community was corrupt and had not the mind to change.

History noted that the Kidderminster principle was the preaching of the Gospel and the consistency of holy living that changed that community. McMullen continues to write that we should consider the vital role that the "so called" smaller church plays in communities across America.   In every community people need to be a disciple, they need the fellowship of the "Saints." People need to be nurtured, loved, and encouraged in their Christian faith; from weddings to funerals, from family problems to social concerns; from a national crisis to personal victories.   People in every community need the ministry of the local church no matter how small that community or church, these needs speak to the importance of the small church. (21). "As he calls it"

3. What were the obligations of the church to that community? In the early church, it was consistent to tell the story and allow God to operate in the midst of the community. It was to insure that everyone had their needs met, which was done through the efforts of selfless distribution. The Spirit of God in the early church moved in such a manner that each was challenged to demonstrate the love of God by giving of his/her substance so that the needs of others could be met. The concept of giving from abundance continues today through the mission programs of the local church.

4. They hosted food and clothing giveaways whereby those that had an abundance, brought of their wealth and made clothing and food items available for distribution to those who were less fortunate.

I firmly believe this is God's way of being exclusive of mankind. The role of the church is to equip and disciple; here again size does not matter. The effectiveness of the church is based on the preparation of the people called to serve. These persons must have a deep personal conviction to disciple; they must have what I call a church heart and spiritual vision. This is a special kind of worker that is connected to God's heart. This person believes that God's commission to ready the Church for His return must be a priority, not on numbers, but on the mandate. The

Mandate is, "Go ye into all the world and preach the Gospel, baptizing them in the Name of the Father, Son And Holy Ghost" (Matt. 28:19). It is the direct order of the Church, everyone who hears the call to go, should be driven by this directive. The word, "go" in this case means to not limit the perimeters as to where or who but infers that whoever will hear and receive there is no mandate on size, it is the effectiveness in which the mandate is carried out that gives validity.

What does a Small Church look like Phenomologically?

Many have a misconception of a small church. They are often considered as non-growing or non-declining single cell organizations. Some may describe this as a Sunday morning church that neither declines nor increases, but consistently draws fifty or so members. This model may appear to not be going anywhere, which is deceiving when one considers the average church size. In America, it is about fifty as it relates to our society and they are irreplaceable for several reasons, the key reason being the connectional church.

When one considers the commission it should be noted that the mandate of discipleship can more easily be met out of intimacy. So in observation of Jesus' model, it was the intimacy that solidified the value of their relationship for the church. The effectiveness of the Church is in the connectivity. The knowing your role in God's kingdom, for you are the salt of the earth. The concept of salt is a great idea. That says that you can effect change without being seen, yet control the flavor of life. However, the society we live in has to have a yardstick by which we can measure our effectiveness. I am of the opinion the Church's yardstick is the word of God!

It is imperative that we change our terminology, for the preaching of the Gospel is not a size concern, as we remember in the early church era, it was Peter that infused the story of God's love for us, as he shared the fact that the Messiah was given for the redemption of mankind. He preached with conviction and those who heard it were challenged to accept the message and be baptized. What followed after that was the model of the early church, they were small groups that met as often as possible to renew the story of the gospel as they met, they bonded so that they could share the needs of each other.

The preaching of the Gospel is the lynch pin of what man calls the small church. Jesus' mandate set the perimeters of definition, as to what he expected. He wanted us to remember that we were given the keys to the kingdom of God. which was the acceptance of his redemptive work on the cross. Additionally to inform us that the same power could transform the world, as he reminds us that we are the salt of the earth. He taught us to have compassion as the Holy Spirit worked in order to move others to give.

Shawn McMullen in his book, Unleashing the Potential of the Smaller Church stated, "True healthy churches grow, and church growth is necessary, but who determines when a church is growing, and when it is not?" McMullen, further asks the question, "Is it a matter of attendance records, membership rolls, programs initiated, or is there more to church growth than meets the eye? I concur with McMullen's conclusion that only God can build the Church and He alone evaluates growth.

The Scripture has said, "ἐγὼ ἐφύτευσα, Ἀπολλῶς ἐπότισεν, ἀλλὰ ὁ Θεὸς ηὔξανεν·" being interpreted, "I planted the seed, Apollos watered it, but God has been making it grow"(1 Corinth: 3:6 NIV). So, as a result, neither the one who plants nor the one who waters is anything. God causes the growth. (1 Corinth. 3:5 NIV). Note the Greek parsing of the word " growth," it's the present participle meaning although one was planting and the other was watering, however, underneath it all it was God giving the increase in both the planting and watering.

There is a difference between the present participle and the present tense. When an author uses the participle, he does not envisage the termination of the action. It will go on and on indefinitely, or be repeated continuously, (linear action) if it is a punctilio (a point in time) action. When the present tense is used, the writer sees the action as going on to completion. It is not an open-ended action, the way that the participle is. As an example, 1 John 3:8 uses the participle, not the tense, so the meaning is: "He that goes-on-sinning is of the devil." It refers to a habitual action. If John had used the present tense, he would have been referring to a particular situation, a one-off situation. Thus, he that sins [in this particular instance] is of the devil. In this case, however, the participle is used meaning in the planting, and the watering God was giving the increase all alone, and continues to do so in His Church.

Did not he say, "Upon this rock I will build my Church?" Notice, he did not say a small or large church or use the word "churches." This statement by our Lord means more than can be seen with the human eye. In the book Small Is Big, Dale et al. explained Colossians 2:19 by saying, "...says that the body is being nourished and knit together by joints and ligaments growing with the increase that is from God. The words used to describe the joints and ligaments actually mean bonded together." The point is that God is the one growing and building His church. (Dale 74)

In Barna Notes, regarding the farmer, he explained that it does not mean that their agency, "meaning the farmer" ought not to be performed; or that it is not important nor necessary in its place; but that the honor is due to God. In other words, we need the farmer to plant and water the text is not saying their agency is indispensable. However, it must be understood, God could make a seed or grow trees even if they were not planted in the ground.

The Skeptic Annotated Bible noted that in the book of Genesis 1;10-1;11 that the plants were created before the sun on the 3rd day. Yes, even before there was a sun to drive their photosynthesis. Why were plants created before the sun? Some say it's not intended to be interpreted literally while others call it bad theology. However when one believes that there isn't anything too hard for God, that's a small thing. On the other hand, It is the farmer who needs water for plants to grow, it is man who needs to till the ground. God needs nothing, for He created everything "ex nihilo." Consider, if God created the world Ex nihilo, the plants didn't need water to continue to exist until it was pull out of eternity, and manifested in time. The point is, thank God for the farmer, it is God's love that allows us to be workers together with him, (1 Corin.6:1-3) so he must give us work to do. We see this when he says, ask and you shall receive, seek you shall find. He could do it all. Man, however, has a responsibility, so he restrains his ex nihilo ability.

However, if the farmer never watered or planted, God could yet bring things into existence. Have you considered, who watered the manna God sent from heaven, in what garden did it grow or in what dirt was it planted? He is a God, who works together with us. The agency of the farmer is indispensable in the ordinary operations of His providence. If he does not plant, God will not make the grain or the tree grow. God blesses his labors; he does not want a lazy servant. God attends effort with success; God does not interfere in a miraculous manner to accommodate the indolence of people. In the matter of salvation, the efforts of ministers would be of no avail without God. They could do nothing in the salvation of the soul unless God gave the increase. The farmer's labors are as indispensable and as necessary as in the production of the harvest. Every farmer could say, "my labors are nothing without God, who alone can give the increase." So it is with every minister of the gospel. However, keep in mind He knows when to give the increase, but you must pray.

God determines when growth should come. Jesus said …."I will build my church." He will send laborers into the vineyard (Matt 9:38) We have seen the fact that God does not determine success by numbers, however the question is ask, "What about church growth?

Dr. Emory B. James

Chapter 5

Does God Want The Church to Grow

Yes, God wants the church to grow. According to the book of Acts, 3,000 were added immediately, then another 5,000 were added to the Church. Would you be surprised to know the church is growing all the time. This work has never said that God does not want the church to grow. God wants you to discover that this vast organism never was intended to stop growing. Tony and Felicity Dale et al indicated in their book, Small Is Big that God has always intended for His church to multiply, although multiplication starts slowly at times.

Bob DeWaay in his article on Faulty Premises of the Church Growth Movement said, "Since the advent of the modern Church Growth movement which dates from the 1050's, pastors and local churches have been under massive pressure to do something to facilitate church growth." Further, the church growth idea is that we must study man using the sociological, psychological and anthropological insights to determine how to build a church that will grow and a message that will be popular to appealing a target audience. Consequently DeWaay writes, "To meet this challenge leaders usually create a plan of their own or buy someone else's plan that promises to give the congregation appeal in the community. Either the program works," Dewaay says, "or the church is seriously damaged."

I believe that there is a danger that some will not focus on the preaching of the gospel. Why is this? Good gospel preaching has already been determined to have failed by church growth gurus because it appears that the gospel does not appeal to the unregenerate. Some believe it's offensive and needs help, so man once again does what he thinks is best to make Jesus' church grow by offering a modern scientific solution to the problem. Did not Jesus say it would be by the foolishness of preaching the gospel that man would be saved? (1 Cor. 1:21).

"By Church growth measures, the greatest failures of all times were Noah and Jeremiah," says Dewaay. For Noah preached for 100 years, and no one believed him. (2 Peter 2:5). Jeremiah's message was totally rejected by all of the people in Judah. Dewaay continues, "Jonah, if judged by Church Growth standards was a fantastic success, however the Bible does not see it that way," he added. (Article pg. 5)

As Dewaay indicated, "Jesus' understanding of what's important is very different from modern church growth technocrats." The point is when we view small phenomenologically, we realize there is no small church. However, it is true that the gospel must be preached to all people if there's to be an increase in his kingdom. But I agree with DeWaay, when he states, "There is an underlying category error here. The continual increase of people entering the kingdom of God, and thus an increase in the numbers in the Church Militant, as well as the Church Universal and Church Triumphant, is also true. These numbers increase every time a sinner repents and believe the gospel."

Pointing out that the Church Growth Movement is not discussing these matters, Dewaay addresses an important point when he said, "The proof texts have to do with the whole of Christ's Church not the size of the local church fellowship. Further, the Church is growing worldwide continually, soul by soul. The growing or shrinking of various congregations is a different matter altogether." (pg. 3, 4)

Yes, I emphatically say that God wants the Church to grow. Church growth is God's will, but he determines the length of time to add to the church and such as is to be saved. He's the one building His Church Universal, through the supernatural work of grace, and it is steadily growing through the addition of souls, regardless whether in a church, at a bus stop, in jails, through personal witnessing or crusades in foreign countries. The Apostle John said he saw a number that no man could number.

We must pray for wisdom and understanding in these matters. It would be wise to consider (1 Corinth.2:12-14). I reiterate, yes God wants your Church to grow pastor, but under responsible leadership. Why be accountable for thousands of souls if you can't be faithful with the ones God has already given? He knows when to add to His Church, remember it's the Lord of the Harvest that builds the Church, not our human inventions. McMullen said something profound in his book, he stated, "The kingdom of God is much larger than any single congregation, and the needs of our society are far greater than any single congregation can address." (McMullen 119)

I agree with Tony et al, in the book, Small Is Big when they concluded, "God wants His Church back. Enough of the man-made programs, and plans; simple church is all about Jesus!"(91) It's amazing; someone made that observation, it's as if some churches are entertaining one another, the choir is entertaining the congregation, it's called Praise and Worship dancing, but are we really worshiping God, or is it entertainment? I am of the opinion this is not what will build the church, I believe it's the preaching of the gospel and the convicting power of the blessed Holy Spirit. Only as we yield to and obey His promptings will there be unity between the Godhead and the Church, then God will give it an open door where many souls will be ushered in. I am of the opinion the church is significant when it's big in love and big in forgiveness. Is our Father pleased when we sing in the choir and don't speak to one another? Is He pleased after we preach a sermon and then look for praises of men, as our hearts are filled with pride and vain glory? O the big church in God's viewpoint is the church growing in the fruits of the Spirit: love, joy, peace, longsuffering, caring for one another, loving one another concerned about souls and that God's will be done. I submit to you, it's "Big" even though it may be numerically small.

Chapter 6

Conclusion

We have come to the end of a lengthy study, have defended this Thesis and proven our view that a church's numerical value does not constitute success or approval by the Divine. We have applied the proper rules of hermeneutics; that is we have allowed scripture to interpret scripture. We have not taken the Holy Writ out of context and we have searched the Greek in order to address this subject matter with precision.

This work has read the views of such great men of God and Theologians, such as Charles Haddson Spurgeon, Thissen, Virkler and other online Expositors. We have compared scripture with scripture in order to not eisegete God's word and we have not tried to go it alone. Above all, we have prayed for wisdom from the blessed Holy Spirit, "For who is sufficient for these things?"

The answer rings out loud and clear. When viewed noumenologically, the size of a congregation does not reveal the reality of God's blessings. As we looked at the Church in Laodicea as compared with the Church in Philadelphia, we were able to see through David and Gideon that God does not depend on numbers to accomplish his purpose. We wrestled with the fact that the even so- called "small churches" are not small noumenologically but are a part of the Universal Church, that John said, "was a number that no man could number."

Yes, this work has attested to the fact that church growth is God's will, but he determines the length of time to add to the church and such as is to be saved. He's the one building his Church, taking the temperature and blood pressure to see if it's well enough to increase numerically or if addition will make it sick. Jesus knows it's His church, through the supernatural work of grace and it's steady growth through the addition of souls, regardless whether in a church, at a bus stop, in jails, through personal witnessing or crusades in foreign nations. John saw it was a number no man could number from every tribe and kindred. Therefore, we must pray for wisdom and understanding in these matters. It would be wise to read and consider (1 Corinth. 2:12-14).

How can there be a small church, when Jesus said where there were two or three gathered in his name, He would be in the midst? I mean every time a small church meets, if Jesus is there, phenomenologically that's pretty big. We've got to see from God's viewpoint. He gives the church rest, if pastors would look at things the way God sees them, there would be no need to compete, to feel inferior, or feel like something is wrong with you or your ministry because you don't' have a Mega Church. So relax, for you are a part of something great! Listen when he says, "Fear not little flock for it's your father's good pleasure to give you the kingdom." (NIV Luke12:32) Be faithful with the souls God has already given you, stop numbering the flock and look to God.

This is not to say the church growth concept has not given us great insights on how to reach man's intellect or his psyche, but we want to reach his soul without watering the word down. I agree with Matt Slick, founder of The Christian Apologetic Research, when he said, "We agree we must reach the culture in a relevant way, a way with which they are familiar." I see Jesus in scripture teaching, utilizing concepts that people in His day were familiar with; He taught them using wheat, tares and mustard seeds. We take nothing away from meeting people where they are, but what this work is saying is that we also must make sure that we do not compromise the revealed Word of God and we must not subjugate it to cultural or personal pressure.

Two Churches must stay in your heart when you consider the smallness or bigness of a church. I visualize the Laodicean Church as big, beautiful and popular in status within that community. It had a large membership without any financial strain and appeared healthy, but it was sick. God saw that church as spiritually blind because their works were neither hot or cold. They were rich and thought they needed nothing, but God indicated they needed eye salve. Yes that big Church!

Phenomenologically, it was small. (Rev. 3:15-16) Consider the Philadelphia Church, so called "The Little Church," because she was regarded little by standing before men. She was not popular, however, God the Son told John to write "...see I set before thee an open door, and no man can shut it; for you have a little strength, have kept My word, and have not denied My name." (Rev.3:7-13)

As Herman Hoeksema explains in his article on the <u>Church of Philadelphia</u>, he said, "In the second place, the Lord tells the congregation: "Behold, I have set before thee an open door, and no man can shut it." Different interpretations have came from this figurative expression, yet in the light of Scripture, the meaning can hardly be dubious. When Paul and Barnabas returned from their missionary journey and reported to the church the fruit of these labors, we read that the church rejoiced because the Lord had opened the door unto the Gentiles, Acts 14:27. In II Corinthians 16:9 the apostle writes: "For a great door and effectual is opened unto me, and there are many adversaries." And again, in II Corinthians 2:12 he writes: "Furthermore, when I came to Troas to preach Christ's gospel, and a door was opened unto me of the Lord, I had no rest in my spirit, because I found not Titus, my brother: but taking leave of them, I went from thence into Macedonia." And once more, in Colossians 4:3 the apostle writes: "Withal praying also for us, that God would open unto us a door of utterance, to speak the mystery of Christ, for which I am also in bonds."

The purpose of the open door is evident because the Lord would create an opportunity and a receptivity for the preaching and the hearing of the gospel of Christ. And if we may conclude, that promise was in harmony with the desire and longing of that congregation. We see that expression pointed to the fact that the Church in Philadelphia was noted for it's zeal for the Lord and was bent on extending the kingdom of God. They were small, but faithful and purposed in their hearts to add to their little band by the means of preaching of the gospel.

Further, Thiel explains, this picture is of great significance for the church today. For it tells us that the Lord fulfills His strength in weakness. The church of today seems to be quite forgetful of the fact that she is in herself of little strength. While the talk of the day is of money, men and organizations, the church has been forgetful of her great task to bring the world to Christ. While we need are sound business methods, we do not oppose all these elements. We surely may employ the very best methods, even in the expansion of the kingdom of God. We surely need men who will preach the gospel and we need funds, but we fear that the expectation is more from these than from Him, who holds the keys of David. After all, let us never forget that we do not open and shut, but the Lord only. He will use His church as an instrument, but that church must always be mindful of the saying of Jesus, "Thou art of little strength."

Secondly, he suggests that the picture of the little church in Philadelphia reminds us that the church must not force the fruits when they do not immediately become evident. This is of great significance, for today this is often the case. In her anxiety to force men into the kingdom, the church frequently compromises on the gospel of Jesus Christ and the truth of the Word of God by failing to emphasize the essential truths. It feels that perhaps men are repelled by the preaching of sin and total depravity, of wrath and condemnation, not to speak of the fundamental truths of election and reprobation. Therefore, these truths are no longer preached. Instead, a certain shallow gospel of love takes its place in order to attract men and force them into the church. Gradually the gospel loses its strength and true content. The result is that we bring the church into the world rather than bringing the world to Christ. Philadelphia had not adopted this method. She had labored faithfully and saw no fruit. Nevertheless, she had kept the Word of God patiently and not denied His name.

Finally, in Philadelphia we have an accurate picture of the faithful mission church. Mindful of her smallness and her dependence on Christ, she remained a faithful witness and didn't deny the truth. He points out that glorious promises are given unto this church, for the present as well as for the future.

First of all, the Lord promises that she shall see the fruit of her labors. This promise is already suggested in the manner in which Christ appears to the Church of Philadelphia. He is the holy and true One, upon whose Word the congregation may rely on. He holds the key of David and has the authority to open and close. In these words, there's already a faint suggestion that the Lord will open the gate of the kingdom and cause some of them, among whom they had witnessed and labored, to enter in. This inference becomes practically a certainty when the Lord says, "Behold, I have set before thee an open door which no man can shut." Hitherto it had seemed as if, with all their activity, they had only aroused enmity and bitter hatred against the Lord and His church.

The enemy appeared unapproachable, indicated their hearts were closed nevertheless, the Lord would open the door and they would find entrance. They would henceforth experience that the attitude of the enemy had changed. Their witnessing would meet with a certain eagerness to listen to the truth of the gospel. The Lord would prepare the field for them. Finally, this fact is raised beyond all doubt, and is at the same time stated more definitely, when the Lord adds: "Behold, I will make them of the synagogue of Satan, of them that say they are Jews, but are not, but do lie; behold, I will make them come and worship before thy feet, and to know that I have loved thee." There was in Philadelphia, a synagogue of the Jews, who were filled with bitter hatred against Christ and His people. They slandered the congregation and the church suffered much.   But the little church had witnessed faithfully even though it all seemed to be in vain and the door closed. They could not be approached because they did not appear open to conviction.

They met their gospel with bitterness and scorn. But now, behold, the Lord would finally crown their labors with blessings unexpected. Some of those very Jews who hated and persecuted them would be converted. These enemies would come and worship before the feet of the Church, in all humility; expressing in their attitude that the Church is the beloved, the bride of the Messiah and took their place among the followers of Jesus of Nazareth. They may have labored in vain, but glorious was the victory. Thiel suggests the same is true today, "all our works may appear to be fruitless and without result, but let us never forget that the Lord will surely bring His own through our hardest times.

As this work comes to its conclusion, let me leave you with this thought, God is gathering His children and He doesn't care if they come by boat, train, airplane, walk or ride He doesn't care if they come through what the world calls a "small or large" church.   He just wants us to get His children home. What an awesome responsibility of each pastor. This great institution, <u>God, the Son</u> died for and made them overseers. God's plan will not be reduced to numerical favorites, therefore small and large are trivial. So let's get on with the business of bringing in souls, one by one, or 3,000 at one time, predicated on how God adds to the Church.

This work has proven that, when viewed noumenologically, a church's numerical value does not constitute success nor does the size of a congregation reveal the reality of God's blessings. Viewed under the microscopic glass of the triune God, there are no small or large churches. God's Church, even though scattered, is one and comprises the "<u>Universal Church,</u>" in which success is measured by another yardstick, which is, "Faithfulness to God's Mandate."

> *"For my thoughts are not your thoughts,*
> *neither are your ways my ways,*
> *saith the LORD." (Isaiah 55:8 KJV)*

WORKS CITED

1. The Holy Bible, King James Version
   1977, Thomas Nelson Publishing

2. The New American Standard Bible
   2003

3. New King James Version
   1977, Thomas Nelson Publishing

4. New International Version
   1984. International Bible Society

5. Barnes Notes on the Whole Bible
   http://www.Studylight.org/com/bnb

6. COG Writers. "The Philadelphia Church Era'
   http://www.cogwriter.com/Phildelphia church.htm

7. Critical Issues
   July, Aug 2005

8. Daman, C. Glenn. Leading the Small Church
   Grand Rapids, MI, 2006

9. De Waay, Bob et al. Faulty Premises of the Church
   July, 2005 cic/issue.org/commentary ministry 89.htm.

10. Erickson, Millard. Christian Theology
    Grand Rapids, MI 1983

11. Geisler, L. Norman. <u>Christian Apologetics</u>
    Grand Rapids, MI 1976

12. <u>Haley Handbook of the bible</u>

13. Hicks, Stephen. <u>Critique of Pure Reason</u>
    <u>http://www.xenos.org/classes/htm</u>,

14. Hindson, Edward. <u>Revelation Unlocking the Future</u>
    Canada, 2002

15. Horton, David. <u>Portable Seminary</u>
    2006

16. Kant, Emmanuel. <u>The Critique of Pure Reason</u>
    Trans. E.J.D. Meiklejoan
    Pennsylvania 2010-2013

17. Martin, Walter. <u>Kingdom of The Cults</u>
    1985

18. McCallum, Dennis, and Gary DeLashmutt.
    <u>Understanding Ministry</u>
    <u>http//www.xenos.org/classes htm 1-la htm.</u>

19. McClaurin, Willie Mae. "<u>The Issue of Rebuilding</u>
    <u>The Temple in Jerusalem</u>"
    Diss Ministerial Training Institute, 2009

20. McMullen, Shawn. <u>Unleashing the Potential of the</u>
    <u>Smaller Church</u>
    Cincinnati, 1989

21. Mountain Retreat Ministries
    2, July 2004 http.// twarren10@org.net

22. Obi, Stanley, "Philosphical Life and certain
    Teaching About the Nature of Man'
    March 2012, march, http//stanco

23. Palmquist, Stephen, "Phenomenology"
    http://en:wikipedia.org/wiki/phenomenology

24. Quimm W. Jon. file 14.6 June 2007,
    http://www.bible.ca/ef/expository-judges-7.htm

25. Skeptic Annotated Bible
    http://skepticsannotatedbible.com/gen/1.htm

26. Slick, Matt.
    "The Emerging Church Postmodernism"

27. Studylight org.
    www.studylight.org/dic/ved/

28. Thissen, Clarence Henry.
    Lectures In Systematic Theology
    Grand Rapids, MI 2006

29. Tax Guide for Churches and Religious
    Organizations

30. Thiel, Bob. Article, The Philadelphia Church Era

31. Tony, Felicity, Dale. Small is big
    Tennessee, 2009

32. Virkler, A. Henry. <u>Hermeneutic   Principles   and Processes of biblical Interpretation</u>
1988, United States

33. Warren, Tony.   <u>Why was it a Sin that David Numbered Israel?</u>
2 July, 2004   www.mountainretreatorg.net

About The Author

Dr. Emory B. James, Pastor

Emory B. James, Jr. was born on February 13, 1952 in Delaware Ohio. He was educated in Ohio until the age of 13, and then he moved to California where he spent his teenage years and graduated from Dorsey High School in 1970.

Upon graduating from High School, he went on to attend the California State University, Northridge and earned his Bachelor of Science Degree in Home Economics, with emphasis on Restaurant Management and Business Administration. He also attended Fuller Theological Seminary and Southern California School of Ministry for theological training Pastor James enrolled at Colorado Technical University, in the Executive MBA program in 2006. Pastor James attended Rhemalife Theological School of Ministry and received his Masters and Doctorate of Ministry Degree, February 1, 2014 under Chancellor, Dr. W.M. McClaurin.

Pastor James was called to the ministry in 1975 and served as assistant to the Bishop Ralph Houston for 10 years. He resigned to organize his current Pastorate, Ephesians New Testament Church, which he has successfully served as Pastor for 29 years.

During this time he organized the Praise Kitchen, which served 400 meals per month from donated surplus foods. Served as the President of the Fontana Ministerial

Association and organized a feeding program called Fontana We Care, an assistant living facility called the Olive Branch Transitional Housing Project for the City of Fontana.

Pastor James has received many awards for outstanding service to the County of San Bernardino, City of Fontana, and the State of California for community service.

Pastor James has served the United Holy Church of America in many different areas since 1974. He has served as District YPHA President, General Asst. Corresponding Secretary Bible Church School and Young Peoples Holy Association under the Original United Holy Church, served as District Elder; Western District Convocation, and General Board of Elders of the United Holy Church of America, Reunification Committee United Holy Church of America and Assistant to the Bishop of the Central Pacific District Convocation. Presently, Superintendent of the Central Pacific Convocational Fellowship United Holy Church of America, Fontana, California.

Pastor James is also a recording artist; having recorded two projects, "You've Been My Friend," released in 1989 and his latest release, "EB James Live," a collection released April 2003. He also recorded a video entitled, "Celebrating with Family," released 1997. He is currently working on a new recording project.

Pastor James' ministry has stretched from Hawaii to Florida. He has ministered in New York, Ohio, Washington D.C., and Nevada during the last 29 years in ministry.

Pastor James has been married to Venice, his wife of 38 years; they celebrated their 38th wedding anniversary, January 18, 2014.

Venice has been employed with The Walt Disney Company for 38 years. They have two children; a daughter Enice, age 34 and a son Emory Jr., age 30 and two grandsons, Varren Michael Jackson, age 16 months and Emory B. James III, recently born. Enice is a graduate student of Azusa Pacific University with a Masters degree in Education; she is an English teacher at Carter High School and is currently pursuing her doctorate in education at Azusa Pacific University with emphasis in Curriculum Development and Instruction. His son, Emory Jr. attended Grambling State University in Louisiana majoring in Public Administration and Music and has returned to complete his bachelor's degree in accounting with a minor in music at Azusa Pacific University.

Pastor James' community involvement comprises of the following: President, Fontana Ministerial Association (2 consecutive terms 1988-1991); Chairperson, Dr. Martin Luther King Jr. Celebration (1987); North Fontana Infrastructure Committee Chairperson (1990); served on the City of Fontana Police Council; Chairman, Fontana Y2K Celebration Planning Committee (9/1999); Candidate, Fontana City Council (1994 & 1996); Consideration for appointment to Fontana City Council (1998 & 2002); Fontana Unified School District (Advanced Culinary Arts & Culinary Arts Instructor 1999-2002); Organized the Ephesus Learning Center (2002-2003); Board Member of International Churches of Praise (2003); Inland Empire Concerned African American Churches, Chairperson-Prayer Committee (2004); Organizer & Chairperson of the Dr.

Martin Luther King Jr. Memorial Monument Fundraiser Committee (11/2004); and candidate for school board member, Fontana Unified School District in 2006. Organized and opened the Ephesus Community Center (September 2013) which houses The United Christian Bible College West Coast Campus, Computer Center, Family Counseling, GED and after school Tutorial Program. Dr. Emory B. James serves as President of The United Christian College West Coast Campus, Fontana, California.

Ministry Contact Information

Dr. Emory B. James

Ephesians New Testament Church

16380 Merrill Ave

Fontana, CA

909 – 823 – 2310

Website:
ephesianschurch.org

www.ingramcontent.com/pod-product-compliance
Lightning Source LLC
LaVergne TN
LVHW051813080426
835513LV00017B/1943